BROTHERHOOD OF MEN

RITE OF PASSAGE

CANDIDATE GUIDE

Brotherhood of Men: Rite of Passage, Candidate Guide

Author: James F. Thomas

Editor: David Aretha

ISBN 979-8-9900601-4-2

First Edition, 2024

Book publisher: Global Geotechnologies

Graphic Digital Artwork: James F. Thomas

Book publisher website: www.theheartofaman.org

TABLE OF CONTENTS

INTRODUCTION

You are about to embark on your own journey into manhood, a journey that will be both exciting and challenging at times but will also be self-rewarding and fulfilling. Right now, you are poised on the verge of gaining a greater level of independence and self-reliance. However, before you take this step into manhood you will need to be prepared and ready to accept greater responsibility and accountability for your decisions and choices. You may have learned how to get a job, pay bills, and provide certain things for yourself, but manhood is much more than that. Once you have passed through into manhood the choices and decisions you make will have a far more reaching impact on the course of your life.

The best way to prepare yourself for manhood is to learn from the men in your life, to hear the stories of their passage into manhood, and to listen to their ups and downs and the challenges they have faced in life. There is no greater wisdom that you can receive to prepare you for manhood than from the men who have gone before you. A rite of passage is exactly this: the opportunity for you to sit down with the men in your life and allow them to prepare you and equip you for your passage into manhood. There is no greater respect and privilege in your life than to allow the men who love you and care about you to gather around you, celebrate your passage into manhood, and welcome you into the "Brotherhood of Men."

The *Rite of Passage: Candidate Guide* will prepare you for your rite of passage as well as give you an insight into what to expect. Each chapter will cover in detail the completed rite of passage ceremony and the tokens that will be presented to you during the ceremony, and explain the emblems specifically designed to remind you of the essentials of manhood. Take the time to read through this entire guide so that you are comfortable, ready, and prepared for your rite of passage ceremony.

Your rite of passage is a celebration of your passage into manhood. The men in your life are preparing to honor you and celebrate this moment in your life. It is a time for the men in your life to share stories, laugh, answer your questions, and confirm and celebrate your achievement. I truly believe if you have prepared yourself and understand the value, benefit, and significance of your passage into manhood, then this day will serve you as one of the most impactful and memorable days you will ever have. Prepare to be welcomed into the Brotherhood of Men.

To be a man, you need to think like a man.

CHAPTER 1

PREPARATION

The purpose of your rite of passage ceremony is to confirm that you are ready to accept the responsibilities and accountability required of a man. The men in your life will require that you understand and can demonstrate the 4 essentials in this guide in order to affirm that you are ready for the responsibilities of manhood. It is very important that prior to your rite of passage ceremony, you take time to read through each essential, understand what each one means, and be prepared to demonstrate how each one will be applied in your life. Each essential will serve you tremendously as you face challenges and obstacles. They will help you to successfully navigate through every season of your manhood.

The best way to prepare yourself for your rite of passage ceremony is to review each essential one by one. Don't move on to the next one until you can demonstrate you understand the responsibility and accountability that is associated with that essential. For example, for the essential PROVIDE, you will need to understand what it means to be able to provide for yourself. You may or may not have a job already, but the importance in this essential is that you understand that your responsibility as a man is to plan out how you are going to provide for yourself. To be a man, you will need to think like a man.

And last, understand that your rite of passage ceremony is not a final exam or intended to grill or drill you on the essentials. In fact, a good part of the ceremony will consist of the men in your life sharing their stories with you. During the first part of the ceremony, they will be on the hot seat, sharing what they were thinking when they were your age. They are allowed the opportunity to share their own passage into manhood, and how they applied each essential in their lives in the face of challenges and obstacles. This is what will make your rite of passage an amazing experience for you. You will have an opportunity to hear their stories and ask them questions. If you want to know what it is going to be like as a man, then listen carefully to the stories these men will share with you. Prepare yourself by understanding the 4 essentials—it will be worth it! So, relax and get ready for a great time with the men who love you, care about you, and are there to build you up.

CHAPTER 2

THE MEN IN YOUR LIFE

Much of the first part of the rite of passage ceremony will involve the men who have been a part of your life. As I have stated in the previous chapter you are going to have the opportunity to hear their life stories, their struggles, their mistakes, and the lessons they learned. Each of them will share with you their flaws and faults, their good choices and bad ones. This is not intended to embarrass them but to allow you to see their authenticity, vulnerability, and humility. We are all capable of making mistakes in life, but the response to those mistakes is what defines a man.

The men in your life have been selected to prepare and equip you for your passage into manhood through their own experiences, life choices, and how they use the 4 essentials to help navigate through each season of their manhood. They have also been selected to make this one of the best moments in your life. These men are there for you, so you feel loved, accepted, and welcomed into the Brotherhood of Men.

Honor the men who have lived before you, and their wisdom will help guide you in your journey.

CHAPTER 3

THE "RITE OF PASSAGE" CEREMONY

(PART 1)

The men in your life are preparing to give you something very special. If you recognize and acknowledge the value and benefit of your rite of passage ceremony, then this will be an incredible and memorable experience in your life. The following outline gives you the format of the first part of the rite of passage ceremony. The men in your life may include other parts or plans, but this will give you a good idea of what to expect.

THE PRESENTATION

- WELCOME: Facilitator welcomes and thanks everyone for participating in this special day.
- INTRODUCTION: Facilitator introduces the elders by name.
- PRESENTATION OF THE CANDIDATE: Facilitator introduces you by name.
- REASON: Facilitator declares the reason why all are gathered for the ceremony.
- CEREMONY OUTLINE: Facilitator provides the outline of the ceremony to all participants.

THE AFFIRMATION

- THE ELDERS: The facilitator will ask the elders questions pertaining to the 4 essentials.
- THE CANDIDATE: The facilitator will ask you questions pertaining to the 4 essentials.
- AFFIRMATION: The facilitator and elders will affirm that you are prepared and equipped to accept the responsibilities of manhood.

THE INDUCTION

- INDUCTION: The facilitator will confirm your induction of the candidate into the Brotherhood of Men.

THE DECLARATION

- DECLARATION: The facilitator will announce the completion of your passage into manhood and present you with the ceremony box, the challenge coin, the witness card, and any other token or emblem that is to be included in the confirmation of your rite of passage.

CHAPTER 4

PROVIDE

pro·vide (prə-ˈvīd)

intransitive verb: to make preparation to meet a need, especially: to supply something for sustenance or support

The first essential is one of the most important responsibilities to understand and prepare for. As a man you must demonstrate that you are ready and prepared to provide for your own needs. Now this does not mean you have to be prepared to get a job, move out of the house, and start paying your own bills the day after your rite of passage ceremony. Demonstrating this essential means you are accepting the responsibility to meet your own needs. Now it may take time before you are fully self-reliant. For example, you may still be in high school, possibly pursuing a college degree, currently in an apprenticeship, or perhaps in the military. Each of these takes time to complete before you may be able to support yourself independently. The main goal is that you have a plan and are working toward that plan to provide for yourself.

This essential is always in the mind of a man during every season of your manhood. A man may experience a career change, a company downsizing, or financial challenges, and this essential is always on his mind. Support from your loved ones and those close to you in hard times can be a temporary Godsend; however, at the end of the day a man understands that he alone is responsible for putting himself in the position to provide for his needs and often his family's needs.

So, take the time to prepare for this question prior to your rite of passage. You don't have to have a concrete plan for the men in your life to confirm you are ready. Instead, you will need to demonstrate to them that you understand and accept that this essential is a responsibility every man accepts in his own life. Give a man a fish and he will be hungry tomorrow. Teach a man to fish and he will never go hungry.

*The character of a man is strengthened when he has
learned to provide for his needs.*

17

CHAPTER 5

INTEGRITY

in·teg·ri·ty (in-ˈte-grə-tē)

noun: the quality of being honest and having strong moral principles that you refuse to change[1]

The ability to provide for yourself is essential for your survival, but to have integrity is also critical. Why? Our decisions and choices determine our paths, but our integrity is used to direct those decisions and choices. Integrity is like the rutter of your ship. Whichever direction you set your

---

[1]

https://dictionary.cambridge.org/us/dictionary/english/int
egrity

rutter, that is the direction you will head in. You will ultimately need to provide for yourself; however, if you choose to rob people for a living, then this indicates that you are a man with no morals or values. A man with no morals or values is a man whose path will eventually lead to destruction. Integrity is the "Do the Right Thing" when we are faced with moral or ethical decisions and choices in life. Integrity sets the rutter in the right direction and is used to steer you safely away from the rocky shoals, hidden reefs, and sharp cliffs in life. However, the choice to live a life with morals and standards is solely up to you. The men in your life can only prepare and equip you for your passage into manhood; *you* will need to choose how you want to steer your own heart.

No man is perfect in all his ways, so perfection is not the goal in your passage into manhood. Integrity is something you choose to live with in life, like taking a compass with you on your journey. When you are faced with moral or ethical decisions, integrity will help guide you in the right direction. Mistakes and poor decisions will be made in life, but even when you have taken a wrong turn, integrity will help steer you back on course. Integrity will be one of your most valuable essentials in life. Deciding to take it with you and use it will serve you well in every season of

your manhood.

21

*The character of man is defined by the choices and
decisions he makes in the life he lives.*

CHAPTER 6

PURPOSE

pur·pose (ˈpər-pəs)

Noun: something set up as an object or end to be
attained. INTENTION, RESOLUTION,
DETERMINATION[2]

If integrity is the rutter that steers the ship, then
purpose is the map that charts the course. As a man, your
heart will need to have purpose in order to feel fulfilled,
valued, and complete. Without purpose, your heart will
become listless and can be tossed back and forth and
carried away by the issues of life. Purpose is what sets your
heart toward something to achieve, accomplish, or fulfill.
The purpose you choose does not need to be very

---

[2] https://www.merriam-webster.com/dictionary/purpose

significant in order for you to feel fulfilled. It could be as simple as rebuilding an old car, joining a golf league, or taking up a hobby or activity you enjoy. On the other hand, purpose also is as important as taking care of your family, earning a degree, or pursuing advancement in a career. Having a purpose in your life provides a sense of importance and value and a reason for being, and will help you avoid being carried away by the issues of life.

Right now, you are starting out on your journey, and this is enough to keep your heart occupied with dreams and aspirations. However, challenges will come, and in those seasons of your life having a purpose will help to keep your head above the waves. Whatever your aspirations, interests, and likes are, learn to build and maintain purpose in your life early on. Your journey will be enriched and provide a safe harbor for your heart during life's harsh demands.

A man without purpose is a heart that is lost.

CHAPTER 7

PERSEVERE

per·se·vere pər-sə-ˈvir

intransitive verb: to persist in a state, enterprise, or undertaking in spite of counterinfluences, opposition, or discouragement[3]

We have now covered the first 3 essentials: provide, integrity, and purpose. The last essential is the one that carries you through all the storms, challenges, obstacles, and hardships you will face in life. Perseverance is the "Hold on Moment" in life. It is what you will need to have to get you through. Perseverance will teach you that all of life's storms will eventually pass and the sunrise will break

---

[3] https://www.merriam-webster.com/dictionary/persevere

through again. Perseverance is what carries your heart through every storm in life even when you are ready to give up.

Your rite of passage ceremony will not require you to complete any sort of physically demanding challenge in order to demonstrate you understand what it means to persevere. The main goal is that you understand what it means to persevere. It is not something that can be taught as much as it is something that your heart determines to do. To persevere means you set your heart to keep moving forward when the winds in life are pushing you backward. Every season of your life as a man will encounter disappointment, discouragement, opposition, and times when you are treated unfairly. These are the times when you will need to determine in your heart to persevere in order to break through. Most importantly, perseverance comes with a reward. Every time you persevere through one of life's storms, it makes you stronger to face the next storm. Each storm you overcome gives you greater confidence and courage. If you embrace your storms with a heart set to persevere, then perseverance will be your greatest asset to weather every storm or challenge you will face in life. *A man who sets his heart to face the storm knows that he will see the sun again.*

CHAPTER 8

THE "RITE OF PASSAGE" CEREMONY

PART (2)

The second part of your rite of passage ceremony will be your invitation, inclusion, and celebration. This is the moment in the ceremony when you will be invited to take your place at the table as one of men. From this moment on, they are to no longer look at you as a boy but accept you as a man. The meal is the opportunity to honor and celebrate your passage into manhood and welcome you into the Brotherhood of Men. The men in your life may include others parts or plans, but this will give you a good idea of what to expect.

THE INVITATION

- THE MEAL: The facilitator and elders will invite you to join them for a meal signifying your inclusion into manhood.

THE INCLUSION

- THE SEAT OF HONOR: You are to be given the seat of honor at the table.

THE CELEBRATION

- THE CELEBRATION: The facilitator will be responsible for preparing the meals or events that follow the ceremony. The celebration is in your honor so you will be able to choose the food and dessert you love to eat and enjoy. This is your ceremony and marks a significant milestone in your life as a young man.

CHAPTER 9

THE WITNESS CARD

Whenever there is a significant event, a contractual agreement, or a declaration, you will traditionally find a ceremony, a record, and signatories who establish the validity or authority of the event. That is why I have included a witness card in your rite of passage. This is the instrument that will be used to confirm you have demonstrated and understand the essentials of being a man, accepted the responsibility and accountability of a man. The witness card will be endorsed by the men in your life and is presented to you at the conclusion of the first part of the ceremony. You will be able to display this document commemorating the completion of your rite of passage and this special occasion in your life.

CHAPTER 10

THE CHALLENGE COIN

Challenge coins have been around for at least the last 50 years and may date back to World War I. Challenge coins were given to a recipient based on their distinction of service, contribution provided, the completion of an initiation ceremony, or a special achievement attained. For example, the US Department of Defense website defines a challenge coin like this:

> If you've been in the military or worked for the Defense Department, you know what a challenge coin is. They've been an American military tradition for a century, meant to instill unit pride, improve esprit de corps and reward hard work and excellence. The coins represent anything from a small unit to the offices of top leaders, such as the defense secretary. There are also coins

made for special events, anniversaries and even nonmilitary leaders.

Many service members and veterans proudly display challenge coins at their desks or homes, showing off the many missions they've been on, the top leaders they've met and the units for which they've worked.

Your rite of passage is a distinct and significant moment in your life, and the challenge coin is the token marking your passage into manhood. The emblems, symbols, and inscriptions on the challenge coin relate to your rite of passage ceremony. For example: On the face around the outside edge of the challenge coin is the inscription Brotherhood of Men. This signifies your initiation and acceptance by your elders into manhood. The "4" essentials are engraved into four quadrants, signifying the four essential cornerstones of manhood. The compass in the middle signifies the importance of using the essentials in navigating through manhood. On the outside edge of the back of the challenge coin is the inscription "Rite of Passage" with the compass in the middle. This is the seal that signifies you have completed the rite of passage ceremony, have accepted your responsibilities as a man, and are equipped and prepared to chart your own course in life.

The rite of passage challenge coin is specific and unique to the group that carries the coin, to those who present the coin, and to the one who worked to achieve and receive the coin. It is to be carried with you throughout every season of manhood as a valuable tool in your hand that will assist you in successfully navigating through the seasons of manhood.

CHAPTER 11

THE CEREMONY BOX

The ceremony box is more of a token to commemorate your passage into manhood. The emblem on the top of the box is the depiction of a nautical compass. Not only is it a tool used to help one navigate safely, it also helps to chart a course correctly. The compass is also vital for survival, a means to assess your bearings, assess your current position, and correctly navigate back toward your destination if driven off course by storms or dangerous seas.

On the inside lid of the ceremony box is the inscription Brotherhood of Men. It was placed inside the box and not on the outside of the box, symbolizing that you are now part of something very special and you are not alone. Last, the ceremony box holds the essentials to help you chart your course in life, navigate the challenges, and remain on course safely and securely along the way. You may include other important mementos and tokens that hold special meaning as you journey in life. The ceremony box can hold anything that you feel is special and significant in your life.

CHAPTER 12

THE MEAL

At the conclusion of the first part of the rite of passage ceremony, the facilitator and elders will invite you to join them for a meal. The significance of the meal and its importance in the ceremony cannot be understated. This is the first time that you will take your place and join them as a man. This also marks the moment the elders no longer look at you as a boy but accept you as a man. You are being invited by the men in your life to take your seat at the table with the men. The significance of this inclusion seals in your heart that you have passed through into manhood. You are now included as one of the men. The meal is where the men in your life will honor and celebrate your completion of your rite of passage into manhood. The good news is that you are able to ask for whatever favorite food and dessert you want for the meal.

CHAPTER 13

THE MOST IMPORTANT "ESSENTIAL" OF ALL

There is a story I came across from an unknown author that captures the heart of this very special and personal essential. The story is about a young boy named Martin. Every month Martin's parents took a trip to see Grandma and came home on the same train the next day. One day Martin said to his parents: "I'm already grown up. Can I go to my grandma's alone?" After a brief discussion, his parents accepted. They stood with him until he was able to board the train. His parents gave him their final goodbyes and gave him some tips to remember. Martin repeated to them: "I know. I have been told this more than a thousand times."

As the train was about to leave, his father said to him: "Son, if you feel bad or insecure, this is for you. Put it in your pocket." He handed Martin a folded-up piece of notepaper that Martin put in his pocket. When Martin found his seat, he opened the window to say goodbye to his parents. The train pulled slowly away from the station and Martin was alone, sitting on the train, as he had wanted, without his parents for the first time.

Soon, Martin was admiring the landscape out his window as the train was now moving rapidly across the countryside. However, it wasn't long before a group of rowdy young men began pushing themselves around and making a lot of noise. Then conductor came by and made a comment about Martin being alone. One person looked at him with eyes of sadness. Martin was feeling more uneasy with every minute that passed and was beginning to feel scared and alone. He put his head down with tears welling up in his eyes. Then he remembered the note that his dad had given to him. He pulled it out of his pocket with trembling hands, slowly opened the note, and read the following: "Son, I'm in the last train car."

The last and most important essential that you will receive is the assurance that you are not alone. This is the last and crucial part of the ceremony. At the conclusion of the second part of the ceremony, a final announcement will be made in order to share with you one last essential. The men in your life have saved the best for last!

42

CHAPTER 14

YOUR "PASSAGE" INTO MANHOOD

Your "Passage" into manhood is the process of preparing yourself to accept the responsibilities of a man. During this time the men in your life are there to help you prepare and encourage you. Take time to speak with the men in your life about their passage into manhood. Ask them questions about how they planned to provide for themselves when they were your age. And most importantly take time to fully understand what each of the essentials means. Each one of the essentials will help you to understand the responsibilities of a man.

Your "Rite of Passage" ceremony is a once-in-a-lifetime experience in your life, and it's something very special that the men in your life are preparing to give you. If you recognize and acknowledge the value and benefit of your rite of passage ceremony, then it will be an incredible and memorable experience for you. Take the time to enjoy the process and this special achievement in your life.

CONCLUSION

YOUR JOURNEY BEGINS

Your passage into manhood only comes once in your life. Going forward, your choices and decisions will shift to rest solely on your own shoulders. However, your passage into manhood provides you with greater independence and opportunity. At first, this may appear to be intimidating and overwhelming if you are not prepared for it. Yet, let not your heart be troubled. Your passage into manhood is a wonderful process that does not happen suddenly or overnight. Your adventure begins once you have accepted the responsibilities of a man.

After your rite of passage ceremony is completed, you will have plenty of time to explore your newly acquired independence and opportunities. A wise man takes time to prepare and plan his future and learns to enjoy every step he takes toward his goals. Use the essentials in your life to help guide your independence responsibly. Use them to help build a life that will bring you the most purpose, fulfillment, and joy. Your passage into manhood is not to be intimidating or overwhelming. Instead, think of it as the beginning of a journey. As long as you are prepared and equipped for your journey, then take it at your own pace and you will be able to embark on your passage into manhood ready to enjoy every step along the way.